My First Acrostic

South & South West England

Edited by Vivien Linton

First published in Great Britain in 2009 by:

Young Writers
Remus House
Coltsfoot Drive
Peterborough
PE2 9JX
Telephone: 01733 890066
Website: www.youngwriters.co.uk

All Rights Reserved
© Copyright Contributors 2009
SB ISBN 978-1-84924-573-9

Foreword

The 'My First Acrostic' collection was developed by Young Writers specifically for Key Stage 1 children. The poetic form is simple, fun and gives the young poet a guideline to shape their ideas, yet at the same time leaves room for their imagination and creativity to begin to blossom.

Due to the young age of the entrants we have enjoyed rewarding their effort by including as many of the poems as possible. Our hope is that seeing their work in print will encourage the children to continue writing as they grow and develop their skills into our poets of tomorrow.

Young Writers was established in 1990 to nurture creativity in our children and young adults, to give them an interest in poetry and an outlet to express themselves. This latest collection will act as a milestone for the young poets and one that will be enjoyable to revisit again and again.

Contents

Bearnes County Primary School, Newton Abbot
Rachel Thompson (7) 1
Maddie Allen (7) 1
Michael de Escofet (7) 1
Lyta Kerr (7) 2
Megan Lear (7) 2
Jade Smith (7) 2
Will Lear (6) 3
Jake Stoneman (6) 3
Allanah Kerr (6) 3

Cheam Fields Primary School, Cheam
Avanya Prathapan (7) 4
Abigail Crook (6) 4
Morgan Turner (7) 5
Jake Coben-Porter (7) 5
Liam Finnis (7) 6
Scott Clark (7) 6
Rebecca Ash (7) 7
Mellissa Thulasseetharan (7) 7
Matthew Lowrie (6) 8
Caitlin Parsons (7) 8
Arenkan Kularaj (6) 9
Lisiana Dancja (7) 9
Maryam Abdul-Mujib (7) 10
Callum Thompson (7) 10
James Powell (7) 10
Katie Sharman (6) 11
Sarah Barnes (7) 11
James Frederick Barry (6) 11
Louis Groombridge-Wright (6) 12
Laura Byrne (7) 12
Govarason Birunthaban (7) 12

Croft Primary School, Painswick
Amber Fowler (6) 13
Amy James (7) 13
Lucas Nixon-Malaure (7) 14
André Stamp (7) 14
Eve Simonin (7) 15
Harriet McCormick (7) 15

Thomas Ticehurst (6) 16
Ellie Yates (7) 16
Helena Cox (7) 17
Charlie Murray (7) 17
Walter Lovell (6) 18
Emelia Bradley (7) 18
Holly Luke (6) 19
Jack Higgins (6) 19

Drove Primary School, Swindon
Tahera Ali (7) 20
Alethea De Melo (7) 20
Siddarth Banala (7) 21
Shanaz Ali (7) 21
Valinnie Crasto (7) 22
Aashwary Chodancar (7) 22
Stanley Samson (7) 23
Jackie Petrie (7) 23
Fawzia Salam (7) 23
Mohamed Saleh (7) 24
Ayyub Ali (7) 24
Daaud Rahman (7) 24
Charlie McCulloch (6) 25
Kyi Thomas-Pryce (6) 25
Samuele Zanda (6) 25
Jayden Stainer-Islerim (7) 26
Tyler Cox (7) 26
Joe Cox (7) 26

Exminster Community Primary School, Exminster
Erin Clarke (7) 27
Heather Came (6) 27
Amie Chrichard (7) 28
Ellie Parfitt (7) 28
Billy Carter (7) 29
Joe Hartley (7) 29
Jay Evans (7) 30
Jonna (7) 30
Lily-Mae Petherick (6) 31
Cameron Keirle (7) 31
Finlay Short (7) 32
Florence Broadbent (7) 32

Jack Gollop (7) 33	Yolanda Parkes (6) 49
Joe Harper (6) 33	Isaac Woolley (7) 50
Molly Godbeer (7) 34	Adam Forsey (6) 50
Daniel Jones (7) 34	Emily Isabelle Lyons (6) 50
Molly Clarke (7) 35	

Nancledra Primary School, Penzance

Finley Carroll (6) 35	Ruth Isobel Jenkins (7) 51
Lydia Flavin (7) 36	Josie Lee (7) 51
Leah Marie Horton (7) 36	Matthew (7) 52

Laira Green Primary School, Laira

	Millie Millard (7) 52
Joshua Bowman (6) 36	Gabrielle Osborne (7) 52
Ben Lazarus (7) 37	Piper Quick (7) 53
Kenya Bevan (6) 37	Katie Lowena Thomas (7) 53
Brandon Igalawuye (7) 38	Leon Andrews (7) 53
Orfhlaith McCourt (7) 38	Lois Murt (7) 54
Matthew Hirst (6) 38	Lucy Rushton (7) 54
Harry Wilkinson (7) 39	Leo Fox-Williams (7) 54

Marpool Primary School, Exmouth

Pimperne CE(VC) Primary School, Blandford Forum

Ellie-Mae Brunt (6) 39	
Jamie Roy Crossman (6) 39	Abe Stanley (5) 54
Jade Karen Pattison (7) 40	Lochlan Belbin-Grant (6) 55
Amazon Start (6) 40	Jessica Scott (5) 55
Brodie Alexander (6) 41	Rose Beaven (6) 55
Job Neaum (6) 41	Sophie Hurren (6) 56
Jade Wyllie (7) 42	Jamie Lucas-Rowe (6) 56
Teresa Scott (6) 42	Molly Owen (5) 56
Jack Bungay (5) 42	Todd Cummins (6) 57

St Andrew's Primary School, Laverstock

Benjamin Milliner (6) 43	
Joe Tozer (6) 43	
Millie Watson (6) 43	Cassia Woolley (7) 57
Adam Parkinson (7) 44	Anya Warrilow (7) 58
Jack Goldsmith (6) 44	Jaden Oxford (7) 58
Victoria Bungay (5) 44	Mary Kimberleine Reodique (7) 59
Katie Dibble (5) 45	Rachel Holland (7) 59
Chloe Hill (6) 45	Honor Hemming (7) 60
Chelsea Bray (6) 45	Jack Steggles (7) 60
Casey Mills (6) 46	Daniel Marshall (7) 61

Micheldever Primary School, Winchester

	Amy Burton (7) 61
	Rebecca Horne (7) 61
Florence Kate Rowsell (7) 46	Chelsea Coombs (7) 62
Megan Rose Start (7) 47	Amy Clarke (7) 62

Sir Robert Geffery's CE VA School, Saltash

Harriet Elizabeth Rose Greatrix (7) 47	
Jessica Elizabeth Bowyer (6) 48	
Elizabeth Kate Lambert (7) 48	
Izzie Bray (6) 49	Ella Williams (6) 62
Thea Grace Oliver (6) 49	Ciera Pearson (5) 63

Lottie Ryder-Wearne (6) 63
Jack Alford (6) 63

Somerford Community Primary School, Christchurch

Tegan Mitchell (7) 64
Amy Hall (6) 64
Marshall Hill (7) 65
Jack Nolan (7) 65
Josh Pidgley (7) 66
Jordan Evans (6) 66
Abigail Ingram (6) 67
Bethany Taylor (6) 67
Cara Pitt-Hirst (6) 67
Morgan Serplus (6) 68
Sophie McCormack-Forbes (6) 68
Cerys Williams (6) 68
Billy Stacey (6) 69

Stithians Community Primary School, Truro

Charlie Miller (6) 69
Joshua Opie (7) 70
Curtis Hanson (6) 70
Katie Creeden (7) 71
William Jones (7) 71
Megan Brown (7) 71
Neesha Taylor (7) 72
Connie Hatcher (6) 72
Max Van Dinther (7) 72
Chelsie Gillett (6) 73
Sophie Knight (7) 73
Emma Crisp (7) 73
Abigail Northern (7) 74
Benjamin Godwin (6) 74
Oliver Banner (7) 74

Tatworth Primary School, Tatworth

Dominic Swain (6) 75
Benjamin Webb (6) 75
Imogen Russell (6) 76
Taryn Brown (6) 76
Bethany Cheatle (6) 76
Seth Ennis (6) 77
Porsha Hallet (5) 77
Rowan Barwick (6) 77
Orla Proctor (5) 78
Katie Winkler (6) 78

William Steed (6) 78
Sam Pittwood (6) 79
Joshua Parkinson (6) 79
William Cunnold (6) 79
Hannah Pring (6) 80
Sebastian Horne (6) 80
Jamie Reilly (5) 80
Benjamin Warner (6) 80
Charlotte Carp (6) 81
Edward Taswell (6) 81

West Coker Primary School, Yeovil

Tia Cousins (6) 81
Poppy McIntyre (7) 82
Hannah Kemp (6) 82
Emma Homewood (7) 83
Ben Collier (6) 83
Lori Bowles-Webb (6) 84
Joshua Cousins (6) 84
Will McCutcheon (6) 85
Owen Zubel (6) 85

Windlesham School, Washington

Tommy Morris (7) 86

The Poems

My First Acrostic - South & South West England

Mussels

M ini mussels under the sea.
U nusual colours under the sea.
S napping mussels under the sea.
S quiggling mussels in the sea.
E nergetic mussels
L eaping in the water.
S illy mussels in the sea.

Rachel Thompson (7)
Bearnes County Primary School, Newton Abbot

Rocks

R ocky rocks all around.
O ctopus on a rock.
C rabs sit on a rock.
K icking rocks.
S lipping on rocks all the time.

Maddie Allen (7)
Bearnes County Primary School, Newton Abbot

Seals

S eals eat fish.
E njoying having fun under the water.
A seal swimming around under the water.
L azy seals under the sea.
S illy seals under the sea.

Michael de Escofet (7)
Bearnes County Primary School, Newton Abbot

Fish

F unky fish swimming in the sea.
I n the water there lived some fish.
S lippery, shiny fish.
H ungry fish looking for food.

Lyta Kerr (7)
Bearnes County Primary School, Newton Abbot

Seals Swimming

S eals eat fish.
E xciting in many ways.
A ll the seals are playful.
L oopy seals n the sea.

Megan Lear (7)
Bearnes County Primary School, Newton Abbot

Crab

C rabs scuttling in the sand.
R ushing crabs racing through the sand.
A mazing crabs.
B eware of the pinchers!

Jade Smith (7)
Bearnes County Primary School, Newton Abbot

My First Acrostic - South & South West England

Fish

F ish in the sea.
I t is cold in the sea.
S lippy fish in the sea.
H appy fish in the sea.

Will Lear (6)
Bearnes County Primary School, Newton Abbot

Sea

S plashing waves.
E normous waves.
A ngry waves splash on the rocks.

Jake Stoneman (6)
Bearnes County Primary School, Newton Abbot

Sea

S waying sea.
E xciting fantastic fish in the sea.
A fish in the sea.

Allanah Kerr (6)
Bearnes County Primary School, Newton Abbot

Avanya Prathapan

A good girl
V ery kind
A vanya's a lovely girl
N ice to people
Y ou're funny
A girl who is good at maths

P eople like me
R eally helpful
A star
T o be kind to people
H ate bees
A good friend
P igs are my best animals
A nice girl
N athan is not my friend.

Avanya Prathapan (7)
Cheam Fields Primary School, Cheam

Abigail

A bi is a
B eautiful girl and
I s a
G ood girl.
A bi is amazing and
I s
L ovely and loveable.

Abigail Crook (6)
Cheam Fields Primary School, Cheam

My First Acrostic – South & South West England

Morgan Turner

M ummy's darling baby.
O n the weekends I like playing with toys.
R ich Morgan and Tegwyn!
G orgeous Morgan!
A dventurous Morgan.
N ever tidy messy toys after playing with them.

T urns things around to make Mum cross.
U nderstands people's needs.
R arrot my cat.
N othing like me!
E njoys supper.
R ooster booster!

Morgan Turner (7)
Cheam Fields Primary School, Cheam

Jake Elwood

J ake is funny.
A good game player.
K ing of my road.
E veryone likes Jake.

E verybody wants to play with Jake.
L ikes football.
W ins more games.
O pens presents.
O bey Jake.
D aredevil Jake.

Jake Coben-Porter (7)
Cheam Fields Primary School, Cheam

Liam Finnis

L iam is fast.
I am nearly the tallest in the class.
A roll makes me laugh.
M an U yes, Arsenal *boo!*

F un Liam.
I am silly.
N aughty Liam.
N ice to friends.
I like my baby.
S oon I am going on holiday.

Liam Finnis (7)
Cheam Fields Primary School, Cheam

Scott Clark

S uperstar
C an ride a bike
O nly
T alk
T o Mummy

C ats are my favourite animal
L ondon
A liens are cool
R unning is fun
K ite flying is so fun.

Scott Clark (7)
Cheam Fields Primary School, Cheam

My First Acrostic - South & South West England

Becca Ash

B ecca is amazing.
E ats McDonald's.
C lever girl.
C uddly girl.
A kind girl.

A mazing girl.
S he looks beautiful.
H SM is my favourite programme.

Rebecca Ash (7)
Cheam Fields Primary School, Cheam

Mellissa

M y nickname is Melli
E ats sweets
L ikes everyone especially my friend
L ike my baby brother
I like Tessa, Aranya and the twins
S miles a lot
S uper Mellissa
A good listener.

Mellissa Thulasseetharan (7)
Cheam Fields Primary School, Cheam

Matthew

M assive powers
A ctive
T all and strong Matthew
T akes games
H umungous fan of PSP
E ating apples
W orld's strongest man.

Matthew Lowrie (6)
Cheam Fields Primary School, Cheam

Caitlin

C aitlin is in Foxes and is
A lways kind and a good friend
I like being in Fox Class because I have loads of friends
T all as well
L ovely friends to play with
I never get told off
N ever naughty.

Caitlin Parsons (7)
Cheam Fields Primary School, Cheam

My First Acrostic – South & South West England

Arenkan

A renkan is the best boy in the world.
R eally nice to
E ach other
N ice boy
K ind boy
A renkan is.
N eptune the eighth planet.

Arenkan Kularaj (6)
Cheam Fields Primary School, Cheam

Lisiana

L isiana
I s a very caring girl
S he loves to paint and draw
I love apples
A nd I like my friends playing with me
N one naughty is my friend
A nd I will not play with them.

Lisiana Dancja (7)
Cheam Fields Primary School, Cheam

Maryam

M y sister is so

A nnoying and she is always laying the blame on me, I

R eally hate it! I always mutter under my breath

Y ou are the evil one!

A nd stomp upstairs to

M y bedroom.

Maryam Abdul-Mujib (7)
Cheam Fields Primary School, Cheam

Callum

C lever Callum

A mazing Callum

L ikes Spider-Man

L ively Callum

U nusually good at tennis

M onkey on the inside.

Callum Thompson (7)
Cheam Fields Primary School, Cheam

James

J ames is exciting

A mazing

M agic

E ats burgers

S illy James.

James Powell (7)
Cheam Fields Primary School, Cheam

My First Acrostic – South & South West England

Katie

K iss the boy.
A t dance club we learned a new dance.
T insel is a decoration for Christmas.
I f I had a boyfriend I would be very happy.
E veryone in Foxes is nice.

Katie Sharman (6)
Cheam Fields Primary School, Cheam

Sarah

S arah sucks sweets
A lice at aerobic art class
R ainbow red rhymes, repeating rhymes
A lways wanting to be nice
H ates hats.

Sarah Barnes (7)
Cheam Fields Primary School, Cheam

James

J ames
A nd
M r Goosberry
E at a
S andwich.

James Frederick Barry (6)
Cheam Fields Primary School, Cheam

Louis

L ouis is a nice boy
O wen is my middle name
U ranus is my favourite planet
I ce cream is my favourite food
S ummer is my favourite time of year.

Louis Groombridge-Wright (6)
Cheam Fields Primary School, Cheam

Laura

L ovely Laura has
A sister
U mbrellas are used for
R ain
A ugust is my sister's birthday.

Laura Byrne (7)
Cheam Fields Primary School, Cheam

Gobi

G obi
O n the weekend I played football
B oo boo chicken Gobi
I am to the rescue!

Govarason Birunthaban (7)
Cheam Fields Primary School, Cheam

My First Acrostic – South & South West England

Australia

A nts climbing up me
U luru is so big
S nake slips down
T asmanian devil bathing the tree
R ustling trees in the breeze
A rmadillos curling up
L ittle ants climbing up me
I see a dingo running
A nts dancing.

Amber Fowler (6)
Croft Primary School, Painswick

Australia

A borigines dancing in the wind
U luru stands tall and wide
S un stretches all the time
T asmanian devil's teeth so wide, bite the tree, bite, bite, bite
R ound and round the kangaroos are jumping up and down
A corns falling from a tree
L ook, look, here's a shark, what do we do?
I look, I look, what do I see? Ants, ants round the tree
A lligators having a tea party.

Amy James (7)
Croft Primary School, Painswick

Australia

A nts climbing windows
U luru standing tall and wide
S un shining bright
T asmanian devil's teeth are wide
R edback spiders crawling up me
A nother kangaroo bouncing by
L ovely sight on Uluru
I n the sea sharks are eating
A lert! Ants!' said the Aborigines.

Lucas Nixon-Malaure (7)
Croft Primary School, Painswick

Australia

A borigines singing and bringing in the rain.
U luru's dust blowing as I climb it.
S harks and snakes being fierce.
T he Tasmanian devil looking at me.
R edback spider crawling up my arm.
A nts crawling out of my mouth.
L eap, leap, snake leaping.
I have some weapons for hunting.
A ship has arrived, let's go!

André Stamp (7)
Croft Primary School, Painswick

My First Acrostic – South & South West England

Australia

A borigines painting pictures in the wind
U luru stands very tall and very wide
S and blows in the wind *whoosh, whoosh*
T he air so hot as it blows in the wind
R ed kangaroos jumping round a tree
A spider crawling up my leg
L ook, look, red kangaroos jumping
I look, I look, I see kangaroos jumping as high as can be
A rmadillos marching in the wind.

Eve Simonin (7)
Croft Primary School, Painswick

Australia

A nimals whooshing about the plains
U luru dusty and hot, I go there a lot
S piky echidna pricked my arm – ouch!
T asmanian devil is black and mean
R usty tyres on the car, it won't get us far
A nts climbing up my legs – help!
L isten to the kookaburras cheeping
I 'm looking at a koala curling round a tree
A kangaroo is bouncing to meet me.

Harriet McCormick (7)
Croft Primary School, Painswick

Australia

A s I grow older I know more about Australia
U luru is very big
S outh Australia is quite big
T asmania has the cleanest air in the world
R ight to the sun we can see giant grass
A borigines are good dancers
L ight shines down on animals below
I can see a tree growing tall and wide.
A rmadillos are giant.

Thomas Ticehurst (6)
Croft Primary School, Painswick

Australia

A borigines were dancing in the sand
U luru is very fantastic
S ydney is a great city
T asmania is a state I like
R agged trees in the breeze
A nts crawling about
L aughing kookaburras in the trees
I n the big coolabah trees
A lerting ants climbing trees.

Ellie Yates (7)
Croft Primary School, Painswick

My First Acrostic – South & South West England

Australia

A rgh. A redback spider's crawling up my arm.
U luru's hot, but I like it a lot.
S ydney's sights are magically beautiful.
T asmanian devil ready to bite!
R ustling grass coloured like brass.
A borigines talk to me about their art.
L isten, listen, the kookaburras are cackling.
I n the trees koalas are snoring.
A rmadillos scared out of their shells.

Helena Cox (7)
Croft Primary School, Painswick

Australia

A borigines alerting ants
U nder the sea is dark
S harks killing me
T asmania has a devil
R ed kangaroos jumping
A rmadillos kicking a tree
L ying in a tree
I n a beach, surfing
A borigines sing a song.

Charlie Murray (7)
Croft Primary School, Painswick

Australia

A borigines eating ants
U luru is big
S ydney Opera House looks like a boat
T rees blow
R ed kangaroos jumping madly
A rmadillos rolling up
L ittle penguins waddling across the beach
I nn keepers dancing like Aborigines
A n echidna spiking me like mad.

Walter Lovell (6)
Croft Primary School, Painswick

Australia

A borigines dancing in the sun
U nder the shace of a coolabah tree
S o they danced in the warmth
T ried to get a bit of peace
R ound up the moon instead
A nts crawled all over me
L ying in my bed, itchy as sleep
I lay in my bed, comfy really
A nnoyed with the little tiny things.

Emelia Bradley (7)
Croft Primary School, Painswick

My First Acrostic – South & South West England

Australia

A borigines dancing in the sun
U luru is swaying
S ydney full of buildings
T asmanian devils growling
R acing fishes going along
A nteaters are eating
L iving animals are running past
I n the trees flowing in the breeze
A lways it's wonderful.

Holly Luke (6)
Croft Primary School, Painswick

Australia

A borigines live in Australia.
U luru is hot.
S ydney Opera House.
T he outback.
R ude animals killing.
A nimals.
L ittle penguins waddling.
I nn keepers dancing like mad.
A n echidna is spiky.

Jack Higgins (6)
Croft Primary School, Painswick

Swimming

S wimming is a sport you can do.
W hat is a swimming pool slide?
I n the water there are people who can swim underwater.
M ums and dads can help you swim.
M ums know how to swim.
I like to practise swimming.
N ights mean you can't swim at night.
G iant pools are big.

Tahera Ali (7)
Drove Primary School, Swindon

Skipping

S kipping is a good sport.
K angaroo skipping is fun.
I t's good if you skip.
P roper playing is good.
P roper skipping ropes are good too.
I t's fun when you skip.
N ever boring, playing skipping.
G reat for a good sport.

Alethea De Melo (7)
Drove Primary School, Swindon

My First Acrostic – South & South West England

Football

F ootball is rough.
O n the pitch you can move.
O ff the pitch you can rest.
T -shirts are stripy like a zebra.
B ut you can't go outside the pitch.
A ll the players can kick.
L ots of players are good.
L ots of football fun!

Siddarth Banala (7)
Drove Primary School, Swindon

Football

F ootball is very fun for boys
O n the pitch
O ut the side of the pitch.
T ry to score.
B all rolls a lot.
A ll cheers are loud.
L ater they have a break.
L ate finish.

Shanaz Ali (7)
Drove Primary School, Swindon

Skipping

S kip and jump
K eep it up
I t's really fun, come on!
P oints are 6 and your
P oints are 5
I have more points
N ever mind, you will win next time
G et the trophy.

Valinnie Crasto (7)
Drove Primary School, Swindon

Cricket

C ricket is so much fun
R un to the ball
I like cricket
C ricket is best
K eep winning
E nd of the game
T hey won the game.

Aashwary Chodancar (7)
Drove Primary School, Swindon

My First Acrostic – South & South West England

Cricket

C ricket is easy.
R un to catch the ball.
I t's fun as fun can be.
C ricket is the greatest game.
K eep the ball away.
E nd of the game.
T hat's it, we can cheat.

Stanley Samson (7)
Drove Primary School, Swindon

Dancing

D o great moves.
A mazing performance.
N ice costumes.
C olouful frilly bits on the costumes.
I ncredible you need to be.
N ice and funny.
G reat dancing.

Jackie Petrie (7)
Drove Primary School, Swindon

Skip

S kipping is fun.
K oala is a good skipper like me.
I am a good skipper like Koala.
P eople like to skip too.

Fawzia Salam (7)
Drove Primary School, Swindon

Boxing

B ad game
O ver game
X -ray of damage
I n the game you are allowed to punch
N o kicking
G ame is over.

Mohamed Saleh (7)
Drove Primary School, Swindon

Tennis

T ennis is fun, if the game is hard.
E at more so you can win the game.
N othing in tennis is hard, if you are good.
N ets in tennis are white.
I n tennis you have to be fast.
S ome people use egg balls, because they can't find a tennis ball.

Ayyub Ali (7)
Drove Primary School, Swindon

Boxing

B ash the other player,
O ut of the ring,
X -rays because somebody might break their arm,
I t is like wrestling,
N ever lose,
G ood if you win.

Daaud Rahman (7)
Drove Primary School, Swindon

My First Acrostic - South & South West England

Boxing

B oxers are excellent
O r falling on a mat
X -rays are bad
I f you get caught in a fight
N ow they are training
G ood for health.

Charlie McCulloch (6)
Drove Primary School, Swindon

Boxing

B rilliant boxer.
O h no!
X -ray shows pain.
I like to see that
N ext punch,
G ood punch to the jaw.

Kyi Thomas-Pryce (6)
Drove Primary School, Swindon

Tennis

T ennis is really fun to do.
E asy games and one of them is tennis.
N othing is hard in tennis.
N othing is easy in tennis either.
I n tennis you have to be really fast.
S ome people use eggs for a ball!

Samuele Zanda (6)
Drove Primary School, Swindon

Tennis

T ennis is great
E nd of game
N et stops the ball
N ight is when they play
I n the day they play
S ee me play.

Jayden Stainer-Islerim (7)
Drove Primary School, Swindon

Golf

G ame finished
O n the green.
L earn to play golf.
F ive points.

Tyler Cox (7)
Drove Primary School, Swindon

Golf

G ood players never cheat.
O ut of bounds means you hit it in the wrong place.
L ots of players hit the ball very fast.
F our balls is all you start with.

Joe Cox (7)
Drove Primary School, Swindon

My First Acrostic – South & South West England

Seaside Poem

S plashing and swimming in the glistening sea
but the seaweed is tickling me
E xploring in and out of rock pools, catching crabs
but they're pinching me
A nnoying – my sister wants fish and chips as well as an ice cream!
S urfers surf the mighty great waves
I like having competitions with my friends to see who can
make the best sand model
D o surf the splashing waves if you love to surf
E verybody has fun at the beach even if you are surfing
or swimming. Everybody loves the beach.

Erin Clarke (7)
Exminster Community Primary School, Exminster

Seaside

S unny, marvellous, beautiful and cool.
E ating is cool, eating is fun, now I feel like I want to run.
A shell is very pretty, a shell is very cool,
you usually find shells in a pool.
S plashing in the water is really fun but the problem is it's cold.
I love the seaside because it's beautiful,
you can make sandcastles as well.
D rink as much as you want, there's Coke,
there's orange juice and more.
E ating ice cream, yum, yum, yum!

Heather Came (6)
Exminster Community Primary School, Exminster

Seaside

S unny beaches are fun to play on and have a BBQ.
E xciting surprises might be at the beach.
A lways have a surfboard or a body board with you
when you go to the beach.
S wim with the fish and have lots of fun.
I always take a rod with me when I go to the beach and have fun.
D oing swimming in the sea is so much fun.
E very day people go to the beach.

Amie Chrichard (7)
Exminster Community Primary School, Exminster

Seaside

S unshine is beautiful weather at the sunny beach
E asy and fun building the yellow sandcastles
with my bucket and spade
A beautiful day to go to the beach
S wimming in the beautiful blue, salty sea
I love eating mint choc ice cream
D inner at the sunny, hot seaside
E ach hour I have a chance to sunbathe.

Ellie Parfitt (7)
Exminster Community Primary School, Exminster

My First Acrostic – South & South West England

Seaside

S un.
E ntertainment to see the fish swimming in the sea.
A sking for an ice cream.
S eeing the sun up above you.
I ce cream to eat.
D iving in the blue sea.
E verybody having a nice time.

Billy Carter (7)
Exminster Community Primary School, Exminster

Seaside

S ea at last – yippee!
E gg ice cream is yuck!
A dding shells.
S potting crabs.
I cky seaweed.
D iving dolphins.
E veryone happy.

Joe Hartley (7)
Exminster Community Primary School, Exminster

Seaside

- **S** urfing and body boarding.
- **E** ating fish and chips.
- **A** sking for the bar.
- **S** ummer is a beautiful time to go.
- **I** ce cream to eat, yum!
- **D** elicious ice cream.
- **E** xcited when I go there.

Jay Evans (7)
Exminster Community Primary School, Exminster

Seaside

- **S** and in my toes.
- **E** ating fish and chips.
- **A** mazing sea.
- **S** hiny sea.
- **I** ce cream is yum.
- **D** emanding sea.
- **E** xciting sky.

Jonna (7)
Exminster Community Primary School, Exminster

My First Acrostic – South & South West England

Seaside

S hiny sea all the time
E ating some fish that's yummy
A sking to eat fish, *mmm*
S wimming in the beautiful, but cold sea
I like eating ice cream
D elicious ice cream
E ating some shiny ice cream that's melting.

Lily-Mae Petherick (6)
Exminster Community Primary School, Exminster

Seaside

S alted, flickering sea.
E xtremely sunny sky.
A ltogether we play games.
S ky, not a cloud in the sky.
I t's a nice day at the beach.
D ancing with our family.
E xtremely nice ice cream.

Cameron Keirle (7)
Exminster Community Primary School, Exminster

Seaside

S unny and entertaining blue sea.
E ntering the toilet with my mummy.
A sking for lots of yummy ice cream.
S urfing in the slippery seaweed-filled sea.
I love ice cream, too bad, I want more.
D on't go to the toilet too much.
E nter the enchanted sea with my dad.

Finlay Short (7)
Exminster Community Primary School, Exminster

Seaside

S urfing is fun on the beach
E xcellent eating fish and chips
A beautiful sea
S andcastles are great to make
I enjoy the view while relaxing
D on't get lost in the sea
E ating ice cream is funny.

Florence Broadbent (7)
Exminster Community Primary School, Exminster

My First Acrostic – South & South West England

Seaside

S plashing in the sea.
E ating chocolate ice cream.
A boat is out on the sea.
S unbathing on the brown sand.
I t is fun playing on the sand.
D on't go too deep.
E xcited playing in the sea.

Jack Gollop (7)
Exminster Community Primary School, Exminster

Seaside Poem

S wimming on the sea.
E ating all day.
A sking for ice cream all day.
S haring fun at the beach.
I eat fish and chips.
D igging all day.
E at lollies all day.

Joe Harper (6)
Exminster Community Primary School, Exminster

Seaside

- **S** pade and bucket, using them is fun, join in everyone!
- **E** ating fish and chips is nice to have at the beach.
- **A** sking for a drink.
- **S** urfing in the salted sea is the thing for me.
- **I** ce cream is yummy in the tum.
- **D** rinking your drink on the way back.
- **E** veryone, you will see me.

Molly Godbeer (7)
Exminster Community Primary School, Exminster

Seaside

- **S** un, sunny sun is the life for me.
- **E** xcited about another beach day.
- **A** sking for a swim in the sparkling sea.
- **S** trawberry ice cream is yum.
- **I** like eating all sorts of ice cream.
- **D** on't forget to go to the toilet.
- **E** njoy your fish and chips.

Daniel Jones (7)
Exminster Community Primary School, Exminster

My First Acrostic – South & South West England

Seaside Poem

S un, sun, sun is fun.
E xcited for another beach day.
A lways have an ice cream.
S wim, swim, swim in the blue sea.
I love the beach.
D on't forget to go to the toilet.
E njoy your trip.

Molly Clarke (7)
Exminster Community Primary School, Exminster

Seaside

S un is fun.
E xcited for another beach day.
A sking for more ice cream.
S unny beaches.
I love ice cream.
D on't swim in currents.
E njoy your fish and chips.

Finley Carroll (6)
Exminster Community Primary School, Exminster

Seaside

S and, sun and sea
E xciting for every person who goes to the beach
A sking for lollies
S unny place to go
I ce cream shops everywhere
D ifferent people go
E xtremely fun.

Lydia Flavin (7)
Exminster Community Primary School, Exminster

Seaside

S plashing in the sparkly sea and swimming inside the seaweed.
E ating cherry and strawberry ice cream.
A sking for a strawberry lolly.
S wimming in the sea and jumping in is fun, fun, fun.
I like the seaside.
D oing shopping on the beach.
E ating fish and chips.

Leah Marie Horton (7)
Exminster Community Primary School, Exminster

Rock

R ow of rocks
O ctopus
C olour
K ind.

Joshua Bowman (6)
Laira Green Primary School, Laira

My First Acrostic – South & South West England

Jellyfish

J umbly fish
E xcellent jellyfish
L ittle fish
L ilac lily
Y ellow fish
F at, fairy fish
I ggly-biggly fish
S tinging fish
H orned fish.

Ben Lazarus (7)
Laira Green Primary School, Laira

Starfish

S piky
T ickly
A silly starfish
R eal shiny eyes
F antastic fin
I magine fish
S hiny, gold, colourful
H iding from their enemies.

Kenya Bevan (6)
Laira Green Primary School, Laira

Sealife

S ensational fish.
E xtreme coral.
A lovely beach
L ovely sealife.
I nteresting colours.
F antastic fish.
E xtremely beautiful.

Brandon Igalawuye (7)
Laira Green Primary School, Laira

Whale

W onderful creature.
H iding from enemies.
A lways eats plankton.
L ovely type of creature.
E xcellent colours.

Orfhlaith McCourt (7)
Laira Green Primary School, Laira

Shark

S unny sunshine
H ammerhead shark
A lone in the water
R ocks are solid
K ermit crab in the sea.

Matthew Hirst (6)
Laira Green Primary School, Laira

My First Acrostic – South & South West England

Beach

B eautiful beach.
E lectric eel.
A gony from a sunburn.
C reepy crabs.
H oney-coloured sand.

Harry Wilkinson (7)
Laira Green Primary School, Laira

Centipede

C rawling centipede.
E very winter, what do you do?
N ow it is summer, I will see you a lot.
T ime for your dinner!
I nside now!
P lay with your friends.
E veryone needs your help.
D istracted by your feet.
E ating leaves.

Ellie-Mae Brunt (6)
Marpool Primary School, Exmouth

Wasp

W hy do you come in people's houses?
A wasp stings people!
S o a wasp lays eggs.
P oints his stinger!

Jamie Roy Crossman (6)
Marpool Primary School, Exmouth

Ladybird

L azy, little ladybird.
A ll the time you find food for your friends.
D o you eat green leaves?
Y our wings can break easily.
B ite greenflies
I love you.
R ed ladybird with black spots.
D on't you love me?

Jade Karen Pattison (7)
Marpool Primary School, Exmouth

Honeybee

H appy honeybee
O n a nice red rose
N ibbling on the nectar.
E veryone likes your honey,
Y ou make honey for us.
B ee stings you.
E ating all the pollen,
E very afternoon.

Amazon Start (6)
Marpool Primary School, Exmouth

My First Acrostic - South & South West England

Honeybee

H ungry little bee,
O n my flowers making honey for me,
N ow it is autumn where do you hide?
E veryone likes your honey,
Y ou make honey from flowers.
B uzzing busily bee,
E ating all the pollen,
E ach day you go out and make honey.

Brodie Alexander (6)
Marpool Primary School, Exmouth

Honeybee

H ungry bee
O n a bright white flower
N ectar, you suck
E ating nectar all day
Y ellow buttercup, you suck
B uzzing busily bee
E ach time you sting
E very time you die it is sad.

Job Neaum (6)
Marpool Primary School, Exmouth

Ladybird

L azy, little ladybird.
A ll the time you find food.
D o you eat leaves?
Y our body can break easily.
B usy ladybird, can do you tricks?
I like you, do you like me?
R ed with black spots,
D izzy, little ladybird.

Jade Wyllie (7)
Marpool Primary School, Exmouth

Spider

S pin a web.
P erhaps you spin a web in a tree,
I like spiders because you eat flies.
D o you walk on the pavement?
E veryone looks at you,
R eally I like holding you.

Teresa Scott (6)
Marpool Primary School, Exmouth

Wasp

W hy do you sting a lot?
A lways stinging,
S itting on your flower,
P erhaps some people don't like you.

Jack Bungay (5)
Marpool Primary School, Exmouth

My First Acrostic – South & South West England

Beetle

B eetles are black. Some beetles can fly.
E ating leaves. Beetles lay
E ggs.
T iny beetle, what do you like?
L ittle beetle, what do you want?
E at what you want to eat.

Benjamin Milliner (6)
Marpool Primary School, Exmouth

Beetle

B eetles eat leaves,
E ating is important.
E very day
T aking my plants.
L ittle beetles eat slugs.
E ach day I go under a stone.

Joe Tozer (6)
Marpool Primary School, Exmouth

Spider

S pider, you are horrible.
P eople don't like you.
I hate spiders.
D on't come into my house.
E very spider comes in my home.
R acing up the wall.

Millie Watson (6)
Marpool Primary School, Exmouth

Spider

S pin a web,
P erhaps I like you,
I watch you crawl,
D o you like me little thing?
E veryone likes you spider,
R eally where do you live?

Adam Parkinson (7)
Marpool Primary School, Exmouth

Beetle

B eetles are nice to people.
E ating insects.
E very time he goes out to go to get some food.
'**T** ime to go now,' said Beetle.
L ovely little beetles.
E ach time he likes me.

Jack Goldsmith (6)
Marpool Primary School, Exmouth

Snail

S limy snail
N aughty snail, you
A lways eat my plant
I like your shell
L ovely snail.

Victoria Bungay (5)
Marpool Primary School, Exmouth

My First Acrostic - South & South West England

Snail

S nails eating green grass,
N ice snail – I don't mind you!
A ll over everywhere in my garden,
I love snails so much!
L ovely little snail.

Katie Dibble (5)
Marpool Primary School, Exmouth

Snail

S nail – you are very slimy,
N ice snail, but some people don't like you,
A lways you eat my plants. Naughty snail!
I t tickles when I put you on my hand,
L ovely snail, where are you going?

Chloe Hill (6)
Marpool Primary School, Exmouth

Snail

S limy snail, what do you do when it is hot?
N aughty snail – stop eating my plants,
A lmost all the plants are gone in the garden,
I like your shell but not your slime,
L ook at your shiny trail.

Chelsea Bray (6)
Marpool Primary School, Exmouth

Slug

S limy slug, why are you so slimy?
L eave a beautiful trail
U nder a stone.
G ooey slugs wiggle away.

Casey Mills (6)
Marpool Primary School, Exmouth

Hoppy The Grasshopper

G rass is swishing and swaying
R emember I am small and try not to step on me!
A little insect in the grass
S wish, swish, it is windy today
S omething I see hop, hop away!
H ooray, I see my friend playing all day!
O ops, better do my job, goodbye
P opping into the grass, popperty pop
P ink and yellow flowers and a green stalk to hop on!
E very time I hop I have fun
R ed, that's not my colour, it is green, that is my colour.

Florence Kate Rowsell (7)
Micheldever Primary School, Winchester

My First Acrostic - South & South West England

Butterfly In The Sky

B utterfly flying in the sky.
U nder the sun collecting nectar.
T riangle patterns of the rainbow.
T alking to their friends.
E ating some honey from some bees.
R acing through the air.
F lying in the sky.
L icking their honey pie.
Y ellow flags in the sky.

Megan Rose Start (7)
Micheldever Primary School, Winchester

Butterfly

B utterfly, butterfly with glittering wings.
U nder the trees, do you see birds?
T ry to keep your lovely wings.
T hink what it would be like to be a butterfly.
E very time I see you I love you.
R rrr, I've found you at last.
F lies are going through the air but I can see you.
L ying down there.
Y ou go by.

Harriet Elizabeth Rose Greatrix (7)
Micheldever Primary School, Winchester

Butterfly Day

B utterfly zooming around, sitting on each flower as you go round.
U nder the clouds you fly from flower to flower.
T ossing flower pollen on each tulip.
T rying to fly baby butterfly.
E ating leaves all the time you are around.
R acing and flying around.
F lying and whizzing around.
L iving in a cocoon all winter long.
Y ou are pretty.

Jessica Elizabeth Bowyer (6)
Micheldever Primary School, Winchester

The Slug

S limy slug trails in the kitchen, where do they lead?
They lead under the dresser.
L iking all the delicious lettuce leftovers
that have been dropped under the dresser.
U nderneath the dresser I'm eating the lettuce
but watch out, I'm going to come out soon.
G oing out from under the dresser and I'm leaving more trails.

Elizabeth Kate Lambert (7)
Micheldever Primary School, Winchester

My First Acrostic - South & South West England

Minibeasts - Beetles

B eetles scuttle, run and stop in their black, shimmering shell.
E ats flies and grubs and catches them by running fast.
E at and run to catch their food.
T ouch the ground with their legs, run, run to catch the food.
L ay little baby beetle eggs.
E at things that are good.
S cuttle, run, stop and catch food.

Izzie Bray (6)
Micheldever Primary School, Winchester

Minibeasts

S himmering web glittering in the dark night.
P utting the black flies in its white web.
I have eight legs and blue glittering eyes.
D irty black and poisonous body.
E very spider come and do the spider dance.
R ed-backed spider living in Australia.
'I am going to eat you all up.'

Thea Grace Oliver (6)
Micheldever Primary School, Winchester

Slimy Slug

S limy, squelchy slug eating the juicy leaves.
L urking on the ground making a slimy trail.
U nder the grass green and tall.
G uzzling up the tall green grass.

Yolanda Parkes (6)
Micheldever Primary School, Winchester

Scary Spider

S cuttling on the wall, going up very high.
P ouncing on nice juicy insects, eating them all up, 'Yum-yum.'
I nsects are getting eaten by scary spiders.
D angerous predators are coming, 'Quickly hide!'
E veryone is screaming when scary spider comes out.
R ipping and tearing, scary spider's web.

Isaac Woolley (7)
Micheldever Primary School, Winchester

Wasp Sting

W asps can sting
A nd they can zoom through the air
S ting a bee, wasp go and sting us
P opping out of their home.

Adam Forsey (6)
Micheldever Primary School, Winchester

Slithering Slug

S lithering on the floor.
L ovely slug going from foot to foot.
U nderground slugs are looking for food.
G rinning at the soil and worms.

Emily Isabelle Lyons (6)
Micheldever Primary School, Winchester

My First Acrostic – South & South West England

Ruth Isobel Jenkins Acrostic Poem

R uns like the wind
U sually wears pink
T ired of Andrew
H appy because she has a DS

I ce eater
S kilful
O rdinary
B eautiful
E nergetic
L oves purple

J oined Brownies
E xcited
N ot mean
K ind
I s nice
N eat
S uper.

Ruth Isobel Jenkins (7)
Nancledra Primary School, Penzance

Josie Acrostic Poem

J oyful
O utstanding
S tunning
I ntelligent
E nthusiastic.

Josie Lee (7)
Nancledra Primary School, Penzance

Matthew Acrostic Poem

M arvellous
A ttacks enormous tarantulas
T errifying
T erminating touch
H orribly crafty
E xterminating eyes
W orrying words.

Matthew (7)
Nancledra Primary School, Penzance

Millie Acrostic Poem

M arvellous
I ntelligent
L oves her famiy
L onely
I s very kind
E yes are blue.

Millie Millard (7)
Nancledra Primary School, Penzance

Gabbi Acrostic Poem

G enerous
A mazing at dancing
B eautiful
B rave at going up on the stage
I ntelligent.

Gabrielle Osborne (7)
Nancledra Primary School, Penzance

My First Acrostic – South & South West England

Piper Acrostic Poem

P lays rough sports
I am incredible
P opping popcorn
E xcited
R eptiles are scaly.

Piper Quick (7)
Nancledra Primary School, Penzance

Katie Acrostic Poem

K atie likes kittens
A crobatic
T iger is my cat
I ce cream eater
E ats sausages.

Katie Lowena Thomas (7)
Nancledra Primary School, Penzance

Leon Acrostic Poem

L ikes fast racing cars.
E ats spaghetti Bolognese.
O wns a big water slide.
N ever eats peas.

Leon Andrews (7)
Nancledra Primary School, Penzance

Lois Acrostic Poem

L ikes fast cars.
O ctopuses like her.
I like ice cream.
S eals love her.

Lois Murt (7)
Nancledra Primary School, Penzance

Lucy

L ucy likes animals
U ses lots of numbers
C leans her room
Y oung and nice.

Lucy Rushton (7)
Nancledra Primary School, Penzance

Leo Acrostic Poem

L eo loves shouting Terminator noises
E lectric sabre-tooth attacking me!
O minous shadows of Daleks with a bullet coming.

Leo Fox-Williams (7)
Nancledra Primary School, Penzance

Abe

A mazing
B rave
E ntertaining.

Abe Stanley (5)
Pimperne CE(VC) Primary School, Blandford Forum

My First Acrostic - South & South West England

Lochlan

L ovely
O range
C unning
H elpful
L ucky
A ccurate
N osey.

Lochlan Belbin-Grant (6)
Pimperne CE(VC) Primary School, Blandford Forum

Jessica

J oyful
E ffort
S ummery
S pecial
I ndependent
C areful
A ccurate.

Jessica Scott (5)
Pimperne CE(VC) Primary School, Blandford Forum

Rose

R ed roses are pretty
O ranges are lovely
S hort I am
E xciting I am.

Rose Beaven (6)
Pimperne CE(VC) Primary School, Blandford Forum

Sophie

S kinny
O wner
P ale
H appy
I 'm lovely
E ggs.

Sophie Hurren (6)
Pimperne CE(VC) Primary School, Blandford Forum

Jamie

J amie likes dolphins
A pples are my favourite fruit
M y dog likes me
I like Max
E mpty bottle I had.

Jamie Lucas-Rowe (6)
Pimperne CE(VC) Primary School, Blandford Forum

Molly

M essy
O pen
L ight
L ovely
Y oghurt.

Molly Owen (5)
Pimperne CE(VC) Primary School, Blandford Forum

My First Acrostic – South & South West England

Todd

T odd likes treacle
O range is my favourite colour
D ogs are one of my favourite pets
D angerous I am.

Todd Cummins (6)
Pimperne CE(VC) Primary School, Blandford Forum

St Andrew's

S t Andrew's is big so you have lots of space to run.
T eachers love to see you and teach you a lot.

A nd never will forget you when they leave.
N o one will be mean to you. They will always be kind to you.
D id you know that we have very exciting trips?
R eading has always been fun but school dinners are nicest, they are scrumptious.
E veryone has a lovely lunch but
W e all love playtime, everyone is always having fun and playing games
S chool is a lovely place and everyone is always going home telling their parents what they have done at school.
So you should come too!

Cassia Woolley (7)
St Andrew's Primary School, Laverstock

My Name

A mazing
N ormal
Y oung
A ttractive

W onderful
A ccurate
R esponsible
R ight
I nterfering
L oving
O utstanding
W icked!

Anya Warrilow (7)
St Andrew's Primary School, Laverstock

Strawberry

S weet
T aste lovely
R ed
A re grown
W et
B erry
E normous
R ubies
R ough
Y ummy.

Jaden Oxford (7)
St Andrew's Primary School, Laverstock

My First Acrostic - South & South West England

St Andrew's School

S t Andrew's School is a lovely school
because teachers are usually kind

T eachers are sometimes strict, when you ignore them
that is when they get strict.

A lways ask permission because when there is fire
the teachers won't know where you are.

N ew children should be treated nicely like other children.

D id you know that our cook's name is Mrs Cotrall?

R emember to always change books if you've finished it.

E ating outside is only for Key Stage 2.

W hen new children have just started school we welcome them.

S chool is fun because we have school trips.

Mary Kimberleine Reodique (7)
St Andrew's Primary School, Laverstock

St Andrew's School

S t Andrew's is a lovely school because they have lovely children

T hey have a really fun play park

A nd fun things to do

N ever lie to teachers

D id you know that St Andrew's School is a great school to be at?

R eading to children's mums and dads

E njoying lessons and having fun

W orking hard and being helpful

S t Andrew's School is great and fun!

Rachel Holland (7)
St Andrew's Primary School, Laverstock

St Andrew's School

S t Andrew's is a lovely place to go to school
because there are lots of lovely children

T eachers are really helpful because they help us to learn.

A lways ask for permission to leave the classroom

N ew children have Year 6 to look after them at playtimes

D id you know that some schools don't provide school dinners but our school does

R emember to do your reading and your homework

E veryone is lovely, happy and cheerful

W e have a school rabbit called Bubbles

S t Andrew's School is great because we have clubs and school trips.

Honor Hemming (7)
St Andrew's Primary School, Laverstock

Fish

S wordfish have a long bill

W hite tummy

O n its back it is shiny blue

R eally quick

D arts through the water

F inding small fish to eat

I n and out swimming

S hining in the sun

H aving fun.

Jack Steggles (7)
St Andrew's Primary School, Laverstock

My First Acrostic - South & South West England

Animals

P enguins are my favourite animals
E xcellent swimmers
N ot flying
G etting fish
U nder the ice
I gloos are cold
N ot fast on their feet.

Daniel Marshall (7)
St Andrew's Primary School, Laverstock

Sprouts

S taring at the green balls.
P oking them in disgust.
R eally easy to resist.
O bjectionable!
U npleasant smell coming from the kitchen.
T errible taste on my tongue.
S crumptious they are not!

Amy Burton (7)
St Andrew's Primary School, Laverstock

Cats

C ats jump over fences
A nd cats can climb trees
T hey have sharp claws
S o they can kill their prey.

Rebecca Horne (7)
St Andrew's Primary School, Laverstock

Food

T omatoes are yummy
O h it's so lovely
M ostly red
A ssorted sizes
T asty fruit
O utside in my garden.

Chelsea Coombs (7)
St Andrew's Primary School, Laverstock

Animals

D ogs are fast animals
O nce a day they eat
G rowl at cats because they hate them.

Amy Clarke (7)
St Andrew's Primary School, Laverstock

Elephants

E ating away across the African plains
L ong ears flapping
E xtremely scared in case a lion sneaks up on him
P assing a sign to other elephants
H ide, a lion is coming
A n elephant says, 'Run, a lion has seen us, run!'
N ight-time now
T ime to turn out the light.

Ella Williams (6)
Sir Robert Geffery's CE VA School, Saltash

My First Acrostic – South & South West England

Leopard

L eopards are running away from leopard catchers.
E ating beautiful grass.
O n the wild plains.
P eople try looking after leopards.
A fter a while the leopard gets home.
R eally tired and feeling exhausted.
D id you know he is asleep? *Shhhhh!*

Ciera Pearson (5)
Sir Robert Geffery's CE VA School, Saltash

Camels

C amels eat plants and trees.
A ll camels have long necks and three eyelids.
M any camels eat a lot.
E xtremely when they walk.
L aying on the floor, having a rest.
S nookeys are little reptiles that attack the camel.

Lottie Ryder-Wearne (6)
Sir Robert Geffery's CE VA School, Saltash

Zebra

Z ebras running around in the wild
E ating juicy grass
B efore the hyenas get them
R unning fast
A t last the hyena dies and the zebra gets away.

Jack Alford (6)
Sir Robert Geffery's CE VA School, Saltash

Tegan Mitchell

T he best thing on TV is Disney
E ggs are my best things
G enie is magic
A pples to me are crunchy
N ice to others

M y favourite food are wraps
I am good at school
T egan is cool at writing
C ute and cudcly
H ot all the time
E xcellent at drawing
L ike swimming like a fish
L ove going to Spain
  to see my grandma and grandad.

Tegan Mitchell (7)
Somerford Community Primary School, Christchurch

Amy Hall

A nimals are my favourite
M y best friend s Cerys
Y ou can do lots of other things

H ail is my favourite type of weather
A frica is my favourite country
L ike to watch TV
L ike to play Pckémon.

Amy Hall (6)
Somerford Community Primary School, Christchurch

My First Acrostic – South & South West England

Marshall Hill

M y favourite thing on TV is Scooby-Doo
A pples are juicy to me
R iding my skateboard all the time
S eeing my friend is good
H ot most of the time
A nimal lover
L ove my grandma and grandad
L ove my brother and sister

H elping others all the time
I like playing with my dog
L ove my dad and Kate
L ike coming to school.

Marshall Hill (7)
Somerford Community Primary School, Christchurch

Jack Nolan

J ogging Jack is seven.
A pples are my favourite fruit.
C hickens are what my granny has got.
K now how many friends I've got?

N ow I'm good at football.
O ranges are good for me.
L ove my mum.
A nimal lover.
N ever stops playing football.

Jack Nolan (7)
Somerford Community Primary School, Christchurch

Josh Pidgley

J osh is seven
O n the PlayStation
S inging in the choir
H elping my dad

P lay games
I n the pool
D o football
G iggle a lot
L ives on Everest Road
E ats a lot
Y ummy lunch.

Josh Pidgley (7)
Somerford Community Primary School, Christchurch

Jordan Evans

J ordan loves jumping on the trampoline
O range is my favourite fruit
R unning is my favourite sport
D ecember is my birthday
A nts are little
N ights are scary to me

E at food all of the time
V egetables are yummy
A aron is my best friend
N o one is around
S nakes are scary to look at.

Jordan Evans (6)
Somerford Community Primary School, Christchurch

My First Acrostic – South & South West England

Abigail

A lways working hard
B atman
I am helpful
G rass
A pples are my favourite fruit
I am helpful
L earning maths.

Abigail Ingram (6)
Somerford Community Primary School, Christchurch

Bethany

B eautiful
E gg eater
T asting new food
H appy all the time
A ge is six
N ice food
Y ummy yoghurts.

Bethany Taylor (6)
Somerford Community Primary School, Christchurch

Cara

C heese pizza is scrumptious.
A pples are crunchy.
R ed tomatoes are yummy.
A nimals are sweet.

Cara Pitt-Hirst (6)
Somerford Community Primary School, Christchurch

Morgan

M y favourite cclour is purple.
O n August 1st it is my birthday.
R unning is fun
G ames are fun!
A pples are my favourite fruit.
N uggets are my favourite food.

Morgan Serplus (6)
Somerford Community Primary School, Christchurch

Sophie

S illy to her little brother.
O n her DS all cay.
P lays football with her brother.
H ates carrots in her stew.
I ll with headache Wednesday morning.
E ats white chocolate.

Sophie McCormack-Forbes (6)
Somerford Community Primary School, Christchurch

Cerys

C ute and kind.
E ats lots of healthy food.
R ight about everything.
Y oung girl.
S quirrels are one of my favourite animals.

Cerys Williams (6)
Somerford Community Primary School, Christchurch

My First Acrostic – South & South West England

Billy

B illy helps his mum.
I love my mum.
L ike my friends.
L earn lots.
Y ummy food.

Billy Stacey (6)
Somerford Community Primary School, Christchurch

Dolphin

D olphins are fun, dolphins are cute, I want a pet dolphin,
oh yes I do!
O h yes I do because dolphins are wonderful,
because dolphins are big fun!
L ovely dolphins have big great tails for hammering things
as well as jumping!
P layful dolphins are very cute and so very fun! Fun! Fun!
H op high in the air like a dolphin, nice and snuggly,
very snuggly indeed!
I love dolphins and so do you, we all love dolphins, oh yes we do!
N ibble, nibble, they are so good, oh yes they are indeed!

Charlie Miller (6)
Stithians Community Primary School, Truro

Shark, Fish

S harks are vicious and scary because they want to eat you.
H aving fun, fish swimming, fish in the deep blue ocean.
A big shark swallowing a fish.
R unning shark in the sea having really good fun.
K arate shark is moving in the deep blue sea.

F ighting fish swimming as fast as he could.
I n the sea there was a very big, scary shark.
S harks are very bad and scary and very vicious.
H as a shark got very big sharp teeth?

Joshua Opie (7)
Stithians Community Primary School, Truro

Catfish

C atfish are really cute but they can bite,
A catfish is quite funny sometimes,
T he catfish are very different to other fish,
F eel them, they are squishy,
I t swims fast,
S ome catfish swim on the bumpy gravel,
H overing on the soft sand.

Curtis Hanson (6)
Stithians Community Primary School, Truro

My First Acrostic - South & South West England

Dolphin

D oing lots of flips in the ocean,
O n the big and enormous dark sea, live beautiful, pretty dolphins,
L ots of beautiful and pretty racing dolphins,
P retty creatures in the dark, deep, blue sea,
H iding from the mean, nasty, scary, big sharks,
I n the beautiful, dark blue sea live fish,
N o dolphins go on the sand.

Katie Creeden (7)
Stithians Community Primary School, Truro

Dolphin

D ancing dolphins in the light, wavy sea,
O n the smooth sea the dolphin dances,
L eaping down to the deep black sea,
P laying around all day and night,
H appy dolphin diving up and down,
I n the sea dolphins call to each other from miles away,
N ow you are bouncing along the smooth waves.

William Jones (7)
Stithians Community Primary School, Truro

Crabs

C rabs are dancing on the wet, sandy shore,
R acing crabs under the wet seashore,
A round the beach snipping crabs waiting for lovely food,
B ig bad crabs searching for lovely food.

Megan Brown (7)
Stithians Community Primary School, Truro

Dolphin

D ive beautiful and pretty dolphin
O ver the beautiful waves
L ovely and pretty dolphin
P ouncing, dancing dolphin
H ungry, happy dancing dolphin
I love lots of little dolphins
N ice dreaming dolphin.

Neesha Taylor (7)
Stithians Community Primary School, Truro

Dolphin

D olphins are beautiful and pretty.
O ver the waves they swim.
L ovely dolphins swimming in the sea.
P retty dolphins in the sea.
H ungry, happy, dancing dolphins.
I n the beautiful sea there is a dolphin.
N ow there are baby dolphins!

Connie Hatcher (6)
Stithians Community Primary School, Truro

Crab

C rabs have snappy claws,
R eally big, rough shell,
A crab moves sideways slowly,
B ig crabs have massive legs.

Max Van Dinther (7)
Stithians Community Primary School, Truro

My First Acrostic - South & South West England

Shells

S hells are beautiful and pretty,
H ide in the lovely rockpools,
E xcellent, gorgeous, pretty shells,
L ook at the rough shells,
L ovely different shells on the beach,
S hells are all different colours.

Chelsie Gillett (6)
Stithians Community Primary School, Truro

Shells

S hells washing up from the shore,
H er beautiful colours brighten up the sea,
E els looking at the wonderful shells,
L ooking and smiling at themselves,
L ooking around the big ocean,
S hells are wonderful colours.

Sophie Knight (7)
Stithians Community Primary School, Truro

Seals

S he is really cute and looks cuddly,
E els and other creatures love to see these beautiful animals,
A re sometimes stuck in fishing nets and are in trouble,
L ooking at nice things, maybe looking for something to eat,
S eals are really wonderful to be in our world.

Emma Crisp (7)
Stithians Community Primary School, Truro

Water

W aving water, splashing

A nd the waves are calm.

T he children play and splash in the deep, blue sea.

E very day on a sunny day the children come to have a picnic.

R eady to pack up and leave the beach.

Abigail Northern (7)
Stithians Community Primary School, Truro

Shark

S harks are grey,

H er fins are smooth,

A shark is dangerous,

R eally nasty shark,

K illing lots of fishes.

Benjamin Godwin (6)
Stithians Community Primary School, Truro

Crabs

C rabs are snippy and pecky,

R eally crabs have lots of legs,

A re crabs mischievous?

B eaches have lots of crabs,

S pider crabs are spiky.

Oliver Banner (7)
Stithians Community Primary School, Truro

My First Acrostic - South & South West England

Guinea Pig

G ood fun
U nder the hutch they hide
I f it is poorly you take it to the vet
N ice and cuddly
E very day they need food and drink
A mazing pet

P lay in their hutch
I t squeaks
G oes to sleep at night.

Dominic Swain (6)
Tatworth Primary School, Tatworth

Crocodile

C laws
R eally sharp teeth
O ver and over they turn
C atch fish
O n their tummy
D ive
I n the water
L ots of teeth
E ggs in the sand.

Benjamin Webb (6)
Tatworth Primary School, Tatworth

Elephants

E lephants are strong
L argest land animal
E lephants eat fruit
P lay in the water
H ungry elephants eat bark
A ngry elephants stampede
N ice elephants help others
T he elephant uses its trunk to eat and drink.

Imogen Russell (6)
Tatworth Primary School, Tatworth

Gerbil

G erbils are funny
E at seeds
R un fast
B ite your fingers
I f you put them near their face
L ovely pet.

Taryn Brown (6)
Tatworth Primary School, Tatworth

Slugs

S limy and slippy
L onely
U gly
G ross.

Bethany Cheatle (6)
Tatworth Primary School, Tatworth

My First Acrostic - South & South West England

Donkey

D onkeys eat grass
O n the field
N oisy
K ick their hooves
E e-ore
Y ou can stroke them.

Seth Ennis (6)
Tatworth Primary School, Tatworth

Kitten

K ittens are furry
I n the basket
T iny kittens are so nice
T iny weeny kittens
E at kitten food
N ice and cute.

Porsha Hallet (5)
Tatworth Primary School, Tatworth

Lizard

L ies on the ground
I like sleeping
Z apping tongue
A lways watching
R uns fast
D ragon lizard.

Rowan Barwick (6)
Tatworth Primary School, Tatworth

Puppy

P uppies like cog biscuits
U p and down and all around they go
P uppies neec love
P uppies can scratch sometimes
Y ou have to look after them.

Orla Proctor (5)
Tatworth Primary School, Tatworth

Puppy

P uppies drink water
U nlucky puppies eat cat food
P uppies are cute
P uppies are good
Y oung puppies drink milk.

Katie Winkler (6)
Tatworth Primary School, Tatworth

Snake

S lithering
N asty
A ttacks
K eep away
E vil.

William Steed (6)
Tatworth Primary School, Tatworth

My First Acrostic – South & South West England

Slugs

S lugs eat everything
L ike leaves
U gly creatures
G ooey and slimy.

Sam Pittwood (6)
Tatworth Primary School, Tatworth

Fish

F lippy fish
I s in a tank
S wims all over the place
H appy as can be.

Joshua Parkinson (6)
Tatworth Primary School, Tatworth

Frog

F lies taste good to frogs
R ibbity frog
O n a lily pad
G oes in the water.

William Cunnold (6)
Tatworth Primary School, Tatworth

Dog

D ogs drink out of dishes
O verweight dogs
G et walks
S o they can get fit.

Hannah Pring (6)
Tatworth Primary School, Tatworth

Dog

D almatian is a spotty dog
O verweight dogs
G iant dog.

Sebastian Horne (6)
Tatworth Primary School, Tatworth

Bat

B ats are scary
A nnoying
T iny creatures.

Jamie Reilly (5)
Tatworth Primary School, Tatworth

Cat

C ats can scratch
A nd cats purr when they are happy
T hey run very fast.

Benjamin Warner (6)
Tatworth Primary School, Tatworth

My First Acrostic - South & South West England

Dog

D iving
O ver rocks they jump
G ive a dog a bone.

Charlotte Carp (6)
Tatworth Primary School, Tatworth

Cats

C ats can scratch
A cat can run pretty fast
T hey catch mice for tea.

Edward Taswell (6)
Tatworth Primary School, Tatworth

Seaside

S ea is fun to play in.
E veryone is having fun.
A ll the time I have an ice cream.
S and in your food.
I lick ice cream.
D olphin splashing at me.
E veryone is having fun.

Tia Cousins (6)
West Coker Primary School, Yeovil

Seaside

S hells buried in the sand.
E ating ice cream on the beach.
A ll the adults do is sunbathe.
S eaweed on the rocks.
I love ice cream.
D elicious ice lollies.
E veryone eating ice cream.

Poppy McIntyre (7)
West Coker Primary School, Yeovil

Seaside

S unbathing in the sun.
E ats fish and chips.
A ll the children having fun.
S and in your food, yuck!
I ce cream is delicious.
D olphins splashing at me.
E veryone is having fun.

Hannah Kemp (6)
West Coker Primary School, Yeovil

My First Acrostic - South & South West England

Seaside

S plashing is fun when you go to the seaside
E veryone is happy and having fun
A n ice cream is yum, yum, yum
S easides are fun and good
I love the seaside, every time I go there
D onkey rides are fabulous
E very day I think about the seaside.

Emma Homewood (7)
West Coker Primary School, Yeovil

Seaside

S eas can be suitable for anyone
E at fresh ice creams
A ll the time boats go on the sea
S ome rich people go on tour boats
I t is freezing when you go in
D ivers look at coral reefs under the sea
E very day fishing boats fish.

Ben Collier (6)
West Coker Primary School, Yeovil

Seaside

S eagulls are flying in the sky.
E at chips on the beach.
A t the seaside I went in the sea.
S andwiches are yummy to eat.
I n the morning I play in the sea.
D ipping our feet in the water.
E ating yummy food.

Lori Bowles-Webb (6)
West Coker Primary School, Yeovil

Seaside

S ea is nice to play in.
E ating burgers.
A ll the children are playing.
S eagulls are squawking.
I ce creams are yummy.
D onkey rides are fun.
E veryone is having a good time.

Joshua Cousins (6)
West Coker Primary School, Yeovil

My First Acrostic – South & South West England

Seaside

S ea is good for swimming in.
E ating ice cream, yummy.
A ll the children are playing
S and in food, yucky!
I ce cream is super
D onkey rides are really fun.
E veryone is sunbathing.

Will McCutcheon (6)
West Coker Primary School, Yeovil

Seaside

S ea is fun to play in.
E veryone is having fun.
A ll the dogs are having fun.
S and in your hair!
I t is freezing when you get in.
D ogs swim in the sea.
E verybody having fun.

Owen Zubel (6)
West Coker Primary School, Yeovil

Shark

S harks swim fast, very fast.
H ave you ever seen a shark?
A *arrgghh!*
R *un!*
K ing of the sea!

Tommy Morris (7)
Windlesham School, Washington

My First Acrostic – South & South West England

Young Writers Information

We hope you have enjoyed reading this book - and that you will continue to enjoy it in the coming years.

If you like reading and writing poetry drop us a line, or give us a call, and we'll send you a free information pack.

Alternatively if you would like to order further copies of this book or any of our other titles, then please give us a call or log onto our website at www.youngwriters.co.uk.

Young Writers Information
Remus House
Coltsfoot Drive
Peterborough
PE2 9JX
(01733) 890066